PENGUINS

of the Galápagos

Carol A. Amato
Illustrated by David Wenzel

BARRON'S

Acknowledgements

Many thanks to Kyra Mills, biologist and Galápagos penguin researcher at the University of California at Irvine, for her generous and enthusiastic help. Without her guidance, this book could not have been written.

I am also greatly indebted to Johanna Barry and Susana Struve of the Darwin Foundation for their help in my search for elusive details.

Text © Copyright 1996 by Carol A. Amato
Illustrations © Copyright 1996 by David Wenzel

All inquiries should be addressed to:
Barron's Educational Series, Inc.
250 Wireless Boulevard
Hauppauge, New York 11788

International Standard Book No. 0-8120-9313-5

Library of Congress Catalog Card No. 95-51837
Library of Congress Cataloging-in-Publication Data

Amato, Carol A.
    Penguins of the Galápagos / by Carol A. Amato ;
      p. cm.—(Young readers' series)
    Summary: A young boy goes to the Galápagos Islands and learns about the penguins and other wildlife that live there and the importance of wildlife conservation.
    ISBN 0-8120-9313-5
    1. Penguins—Galápagos Islands—Juvenile literature. 2. Natural history—Galápagos Islands—Juvenile literature. 3. Galápagos Islands—Juvenile literature.
[1. Penguins. 2. Natural history—Galápagos Islands. 3. Galápagos Islands. 4. Wildlife conservation.] I. Title. II. Series: Amato, Carol A. Young readers series.
    QL696.S473A46 1996
    598.4'41'098665—dc20
                       95-51837
                       CIP
                       AC

PRINTED IN HONG KONG
987654321

Table of Contents

"Jesse, look below," said his mother. "You can see the Galápagos Islands. We're here, at last! Soon we will see the penguins!"

Jesse looked down through patches of dark clouds.

"Awesome!" he said. "How many islands are there, Mom? How did they get there?"

"Oh my. One question at a time!" laughed his mother. "There are thirteen big islands, six small ones, and even smaller ones called islets. The islands are the tops of huge volcanoes."

"Volcanoes in the sea?" asked Jesse.

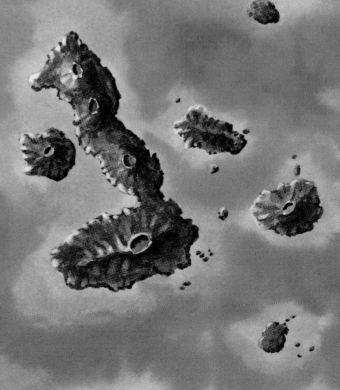

"Yes," said his mother, "volcanoes can be on the land or in the sea. These islands were formed millions of years ago. Hot, melted rock called lava burst up through openings in the ocean floor. The volcanoes burst, or erupted, many times. The lava hardened as it cooled. After a long time, the piled up lava formed these islands. Some of the volcanoes here still erupt."

"I hope they won't erupt near us!" exclaimed Jesse.

"Don't worry, Jesse! Scientists use special instruments to find out if a volcano is ready to erupt. They can often tell this about a week before it happens."

Jesse's mother, Jo, is a marine biologist. Marine biologists research, or study, about life in the sea. She is now doing research about the Galápagos penguin, one of the seabirds on the islands. Jesse has been allowed to go with her to observe, or look, at the penguins. His mother hopes her research will help others to learn how to protect the penguin.

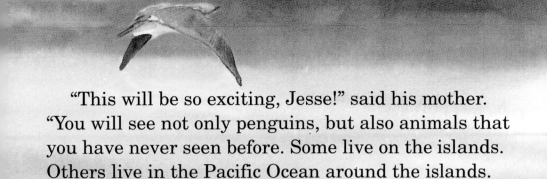

"This will be so exciting, Jesse!" said his mother.
"You will see not only penguins, but also animals that
you have never seen before. Some live on the islands.
Others live in the Pacific Ocean around the islands.
Amazing birds fill the sky."

"But Mom, how did the plants, penguins, and other
animals get way out here?" asked Jesse.

"That's a good question," said his mother. "No one
knows for sure. Plants could have been brought by the
wind. Seeds may have stuck to the wings of birds or
come on the ocean waves. The reptiles may have come
on rafts of tangled plants and weeds. Others could fly.
Some animals may have come from nearby islands that
disappeared into the sea long ago. The animals may
have been able to swim here. The Galápagos are 600
miles (1,016 kilometers) from South America!"

"That would have been a long trip, if they came from
South America!" said Jesse.

The plane landed at the small airport on the island of Santa Cruz.

"We must take a bus to the Charles Darwin Research Station," said Jesse's mother. "We will stay there during our visit."

"Who's Charles Darwin?" asked Jesse.

"Long ago, a naturalist named Charles Darwin did research on these islands," explained Jo. "A naturalist studies about nature. Darwin later became famous for his ideas about how animals make changes so they can survive."

Soon they arrived. Inside the research station, a man and a young girl walked up to them.

"Carlos!" said Jesse's mother. "I haven't seen you in so long!" They hugged one another warmly.

"This is my son, Jesse," said his mother. "Jesse, Carlos is a naturalist. He lives in the Galápagos. Carlos knows many things about the plants and animals here. He will also be our guide."

"And this is my daughter, Carmen," said Carlos. "Carmen is learning many things here."

The children smiled at one another.

"Papi, can I take Jesse outside?" asked Carmen.

"Sure," said her father.

The children walked along a path near the station.

"You and your mother will be staying over there," Carmen said, pointing to a nearby building. "That's where visiting scientists live while they work in the Galápagos."

"Why do they have a research station here, Carmen?" Jesse asked.

"Scientists research about the plants and animals here," said Carmen. "By learning, they can try to plan ways to keep living things protected on the Galápagos. These islands are very, very special. You'll see why soon!"

"Carmen! It's time to go," called Carlos. The children went inside.

"I have chartered a boat for our island trips," said Carlos. "Carmen and I will come for you bright and early."

"We'll be ready!" said Jo.

The next day, they left before sunrise for the tiny island of Bartolomé. Here they hoped to find a small colony, or group, of penguins.

"Look!" shouted Carmen from the bow of the boat. "I can see the island. There's Pinnacle Rock."

The boat took them to the Bartolomé shore.

Soon they were walking on a wooden stairway up the steep lava rocks of a volcano.

"Phew, it's warm here," said Jesse. "I thought penguins lived in cold places."

"The cold-weather penguins do, Jesse," said his mother. "Galápagos penguins are warm-weather penguins. In fact, both cold- and warm-weather penguins live in southern parts of the world."

"I thought penguins lived way up north near polar bears," said Jesse.

"Many people think they do," said his mother. "There are no penguins in the North. Penguins can't fly, so they can't travel to the North."

"Why can't they fly, Mom?" asked Jesse.

"Millions of years ago, penguins were flying birds," explained Jo. "Many of them flew to Antarctica, which is over the South Pole. Antarctica was a warm place then. There was plenty of food for the penguins. They stopped flying to other places. In time, their wings became more like flippers to 'fly' through the sea. Today Antarctica is covered with snow and ice and is the home of the cold-weather penguins."

The day was getting warmer. They stopped to rest.

"Papi," said Carmen. "How many kinds of penguins are there?"

"Well, Carmen," said her father, "there are eighteen different species, or kinds, of penguins. The largest ones live near the South Pole where it's very cold. The smallest live near the equator where it is very warm. They swim in the cool flowing water, or currents, here. There's a lot of food for the sea animals in these currents."

GENTOO

CHINSTRAP

MACARON

GALÁPAGOS

12

"What's the equator, Carlos?" asked Jesse.

"It's like a circle around the earth," answered Carlos. "You can't see the equator. We just use this word to divide the earth into two parts. Above the equator are the northern parts. Below it are the southern parts."

The group began walking again. Lava lizards were everywhere. Sally Lightfoot crabs popped up looking like bright red spots on the dark lava rocks. At last they reached the top of the volcano.

"Wow!" said Jesse, looking out across the rocks and the sea. "This looks like another world!"

EMPEROR

North America

Galápagos Islands

South America

Equator

JACKASS

Antarctica

ADÉLIE

13

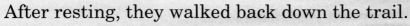

After resting, they walked back down the trail.

"Look!" exclaimed Carmen. "I see a group of penguins. They weren't there before. They're standing outside those lava caves."

"They were probably out fishing this morning," said Jo. "They spend most of their day in the sea."

"They're so small," said Jesse, "that they look like stuffed animal toys!"

"They do, Jesse," said Carlos. "They are the second smallest penguins, about twenty-one inches (53.34 centimeters) tall. They weigh about five pounds (2.3 kilograms) or so. The males (boys) are

bigger than the females (girls), but it is hard to see other differences."

"Why are they all facing the same way with their wings out?" asked Jesse.

"They're cooling off," answered his mother. "They face the breeze and lift up their wings. This lets the warm air escape from their bodies. On sunny days, they stay in the caves to keep cool. Their underfeathers are like a down jacket. Even cold-weather penguins must cool off after they have been active."

"And," said Carlos, "a penguin has from 70 to 200 feathers on every inch of its body!"

"That's some jacket!" said Jesse.

Suddenly, several of the tiny penguins walked toward them. While they looked clumsy as they wobbled on their short legs, they could move easily and quickly across the rocks.

"We're being attacked!" shouted Jesse, hiding behind his mother. The others laughed. The penguins circled around them.

"Don't worry," said Carlos. "The penguins here are tame and friendly. They are used to people, since so many come here. On some of the other islands, they are very shy. You will see, Jesse, that the animals of the Galápagos are not afraid of people."

"Why not?" asked Jesse.

"Well," began Carlos, "this is a bit of a story. For many years, no one knew about the Galápagos. Then people discovered the islands. They saw that the animals were very friendly. The animals had no reason to fear people. Some people hunted the animals, but the animals were still friendly. Now there are laws about hunting and fishing. People live on some of these islands. We try to help them understand why the animals on land and in the sea must be protected. If too many are hunted, some species of animals will die out. Also, thousands of other people come to visit the islands each year. If people hunt or bother the animals too much, the Galápagos will be changed forever."

One little penguin walked right up to Carmen. It looked her over, up and down.

"Either it's very nosy, or it can't see very well!" laughed Carmen.

"It may be a little bit of both," said Jo. "Biologists are still studying the Galápagos penguin's eyesight. We are not sure how well these penguins see on land, but we do think that they see very well in the water."

"What a long bill you have," Carmen said to the penguin.

"The better to eat you with, my dear," growled Carlos. "Really, its bill is as sharp as a knife so it can protect itself."

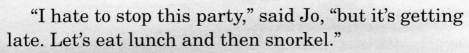

"I hate to stop this party," said Jo, "but it's getting late. Let's eat lunch and then snorkel."

"So long, penguins," said Jesse as they turned to go.

"I wish I could take this one home with me," said Carmen. The little penguin followed her for a few steps. Then the penguin puffed up its chest, raised its wings, and lifted its head toward the sky. It let out a strange sound.

"What's that?" asked Jesse.

"That's penguin talk," laughed Carlos.

"It sounds more like a donkey," said Jesse. "What a big sound for such a little bird!"

"That's why their family, or species, of penguins, are called the Jackass penguins," said Jo. "We think the braying sound is used mostly when the males and females are together. They usually bray in the early morning and at night, especially on moonlit nights. The penguins also make a short call when they want to locate one another. All penguins move their bodies in ways that tell how they feel."

Everyone walked to the boat to get lunch and snorkeling gear.

"I have a question, Mom," Jesse said as he ate. "Do other animals hunt these penguins?"

"Yes," said his mother. "Snakes, rice rats, and hawks hunt their eggs and small chicks. Cats, dogs, and other animals hunt them on some islands. The cats and dogs were brought by people who came to live here. Some of them became wild. They're a big problem for many of the animals that are native to these islands."

After lunch and a rest, everyone
put on masks and fins.

"Last one in is a penguin that sounds
like a donkey!" said Jesse, as he headed
for the water. He was the first to start snorkeling.

"Oh my gosh!" he said, looking beneath the water.
"I've never seen so many amazing creatures!"

"Hey, everyone," called Carmen. "I can see penguins
swimming underwater." They all looked underwater, too.

"They're swimming so fast, it seems like they're
flying through the water!" said Jesse. "They look
like torpedoes!"

"They do, Jesse," said Jo. "Underwater, some
penguins can swim up to twenty-five miles
(40 kilometers) an hour. Watch them pump their
stubby tails and webbed feet. They use them to steer."

"One just dove next to me," said Carmen. "Papi,
how long can a penguin hold its breath underwater?"

"For over a minute," said her father, "but most of their dives are not deep here in Bartolomé. We will visit Fernandina Island where penguins have been observed to dive deeper. That one near Jesse is swimming on top of the water! It uses its flippers like paddles. It's not surprising that penguins spend most of their time in the water."

"Look at the penguins out there, everyone," said Carmen. "They're leaping, or porpoising, in and out of the water like dolphins!"

"Sharks! Sharks!" Jesse suddenly yelled. "I can see lots of sharks out there," he said pointing out toward the deeper water.

"Don't worry, Jesse," said Carlos. "Those are white-tipped sharks. People can swim near them, and they won't attack."

"These *are* magical islands!" said Jesse.

"And we have more magic to see," said his mother. "It's time to leave for the next part of our trip."

On the beach, they all took off their snorkeling gear. At the other end of the beach, a group of sea lions were also leaving the water. Jesse and Carmen ran along the shore to see them.

"I'll race you!" Jesse said to Carmen. He reached the sea lions before Carmen. A sea lion pup came right up to them.

"I can't believe all of this," said Jesse. "Penguins that sound like donkeys, safe sharks, and friendly sea lions! What's next?"

Chapter **6** Fernandina Island

The tired but happy explorers boarded the boat. The setting sun cast a golden light on Pinnacle Rock. They were traveling next to the island of Fernandina to see a larger colony of penguins. The penguins usually breed and raise their chicks on Fernandina and on another nearby island.

"Will it take a long time to get to Fernandina, Mom?" Jesse asked.

"Well, when you wake up tomorrow, we'll be there. Now, I know what you're going to say 'awesome,' right?"

"Right!" laughed Jesse.

Early the next morning, they could see Fernandina's lava coast through the light fog.

"This island looks like the moon!" said Carmen. "My papi says that except for those trees and the lava cactus, few plants can grow here."

"It looks like a dark desert," said Jesse.

After leaving the boat, they began following a trail through a lava field.

"This volcano erupted just a few years ago. Be careful not to trip in the lava cracks!" warned Carlos.

"Watch out!" Carmen called to Jesse, who was ahead of her. "You almost stepped into that big hole."

Jesse stopped short in front of the hole.

"And also watch out for that dragon next to you on those rocks!" she said. Jesse let out a yell.

"Stop teasing him," said Carlos. "Jesse, that's a marine iguana. That hole is its nest. Look above you on those rocks. All those iguanas are sunning themselves. They eat seaweed and must warm up after swimming. And don't worry, they're perfectly harmless."

They walked carefully along the lava rock shore.

"Why do the penguins come to this lonely island?" asked Jesse.

"Well, Jesse," said his mother, "the cold current here is very strong. It brings penguin food like sardines, anchovies, and other small fish to the top of the sea. When there is plenty of food, the penguins can breed and raise their chicks here all year long."

"How can they make nests on these bare rocks?" asked Carmen.

"It is a hard place to nest and raise babies," said Carlos. "First, the male and the female find a cool, shaded cave or rocky cliff. Next, they gather twigs, leaves, feathers, and even stones to make a nest. The female usually lays two white eggs. Both penguin parents take turns sitting on the eggs, which hatch in about forty-two days."

"What are the chicks like when they hatch?" asked Jesse.

"They are a fuzzy gray, blind, and helpless," said Jo, "but in a few days, they open their eyes. The parents keep the chicks warm and clean. The father and mother penguins are like a good family team. They both share the hard work of raising chicks."

"How long do the chicks stay with their parents?" asked Carmen.

"For about thirty days," said her father. "They stay near the nest until they fledge at fifty to sixty days old."

"Fledging is when they learn to swim," Carmen proudly explained to Jesse.

"Well, then," said Jesse, "I fledged when I was seven!"

Carlos stopped talking and walking.

"Look over there," he said to the others. "I can see the penguin colony outside those lava caves. Let's go!"

Soon they were standing near a small group of penguins.

"Oh, no," said Jesse. "Some of the smallest ones must be sick. Their feathers look so messy."

"They *do* look messy," said Jo, "but they're not sick, Jesse. Those are chicks, and they're molting."

"What's 'molting,' Mom?" he asked.

"For chicks, molting is part of growing up," she answered. "The chick's downy feathers fall out. Waterproof feathers grow in. Then the chick can swim and care for itself. The chicks don't get their black and white adult feathers until they are about three years old. Until then, they look like they're wearing a brown hood and cape. The Galápagos penguin's black and white feathers are not as bright as those of other penguins."

"Papi told me that Galápagos penguins molt twice a year," said Carmen. "Their old feathers wear out like old clothes! It takes about twelve days for them to molt."

"Good remembering, Carmen!" said her father. "The penguins can't swim when they're molting, so they can't eat."

"Don't they starve?" asked Jesse.

"Good question!" said his mother. "They eat a lot before they molt. By doing this, they can live off their fat, or blubber. Blubber also keeps them warm in cold water."

"Look," said Jesse. "Many of the penguins are poking themselves."

"Those penguins are preening, Jesse," said Carlos.
"When birds preen, they clean and comb their feathers.
Waterbirds like penguins must keep their feathers
waterproof. To do this, they coat their feathers with
oil. They get the oil from a place under their tails."

"Look, everyone," said Carmen. "One of the penguin parents is feeding its chick." The chick put its beak inside the parent's mouth.

"I don't see any food," said Jesse.

"Here's how penguin feeding works," said Jo. "One parent guards the chicks while the other hunts. The hunting parent finds food, such as a fish, in the sea. It swallows the fish head first so the scales and fins won't get caught in its throat. The food passes into the

crop, a place at the bottom of the throat where it can be stored. Then the parent returns to the nest. One of the chicks touches the parent's bill with its own bill. The parent brings the food it ate back up from its crop for the chick to eat! What do you think about that, Jesse?"

"I'm glad human parents don't feed their children that way," laughed Jesse, "but it's a great way for penguins!"

"We're in for a treat," said Jo. "Look at that chick—
the one with all of its new feathers. It's heading for the
sea!"

They all followed the chick, walking carefully across
the lava rocks.

The chick jumped right into the sea from the edge of
the rocks. It began to swim on top of the water.

"Can you believe it?" said Carmen. "The chick didn't
even need swimming lessons!"

"It took me a whole summer to learn how to swim!"
said Jesse.

The little penguin dove in and out of the waves.

"That looks like so much fun," said Carmen. "I wish I could fly through the sea like that!"

"And it's only about seven or eight weeks old!" said Carlos.

"I hate to say this everyone," shouted Jo over the sound of the crashing waves, "but we have to leave."

"Good-bye," Jesse called to the little penguin. "Have a good life!"

They all walked back to the boat. A few iguanas were near the water's edge. They moved together to keep warm before nightfall. Soon the boat left the dark lava coast of Fernandina.

"Listen," said Jo. "The penguins are calling."

Sea lions and penguins were porpoising on each side of the boat. Brown pelicans flew above them. Whales spouted in the distance.

"These islands don't seem real," said Jesse.

"They have a kind of magic," Carmen said. "Just wait until you see some of the other amazing animals here!"

"I think we all feel something special here in the Galápagos," said Carlos. "Perhaps it's because the animals really trust us."

"Yes," said Jo. "And we must continue to deserve this trust. We must always protect the magic of these enchanted islands!"

Afterword

After reading this book, you may want to find out more about the fascinating Galápagos Islands. The early Spanish explorers gave them their first name, *Las Islas Encantadas,* or the Enchanted Islands. It is no wonder. These islands are home to some of the most unusual creatures on the planet. There are giant land tortoises that weigh up to 600 pounds (270 kilograms), dancing birds called blue-footed boobies, frigate birds with pouches that inflate like red balloons, and many, many more.

Charles Darwin, the English naturalist, conducted important research on the islands, making many of the scientific observations that helped him develop his theory of evolution.

In time, these isolated islands were visited by people who did more than just look at the wildlife. Visiting vessels called on the islands to hunt and fish the waters. Settlers came to live on four of the islands, fishing the waters, farming the land, and bringing new animals that threatened the extraordinary local animals.

By 1990, there were more than 12,000 people living on the islands, and many times more who came as tourists to visit them. As we learned in the story, laws to protect the Galápagos wildlife were passed. Today these laws cannot always be enforced. In time, these wonderful, friendly creatures may be endangered and even face extinction. We must all learn to work to protect the Galápagos animals and their world so that future generations may be allowed to be enchanted by them.

Glossary

Antarctica (Ant-ARC-ti-ca) the continent around the South Pole. Antarctica is almost completely surrounded by a huge ice sheet.

Bartolomé Island (Bar-tol-o-ME I {s}-land) a small island off the shore of the much larger San Salvador Island in the Galápagos.

bill a bird's beak or mouthpart.

biologist (bi-OL-o-gist) a scientist who studies plant and animal life.

breeding (BREED-ing) the time when mating between male and female animals takes place in order to produce young.

brown pelican (brown PEL-i-can) a seabird that dives for fish. It catches the fish in a pouch that is attached to its long bill.

Charles Darwin Research Station (Charles DAR-win RE-search STA-tion) is located on the island of Santa Cruz in the Galápagos. Scientists there gather information about the Galápagos plants and animals. The Galápagos National Park Service makes sure plans to protect the living things there are carried out. The research station was named after Charles Darwin. He was one of the first naturalists to do important research about the Galápagos.

charter (CHAR-ter) to hire, or rent. Many of the scientists who do research in the Galápagos Islands hire fishing boats to take them to the islands.

island (I {s}-land) land that is surrounded by water.

lava lizards (LA-va LIZ-ards) the four- to eight-inch (10- to 20-centimeter) lizards that run in and out of the lava cracks on many of the Galápagos Islands. They are very tame.

marine biologist (mar-INE bi-OL-o-gist) a scientist who studies the oceans and the life in them.

naturalist (NAT-ur-al-list) someone who studies the science and nature of living things.

Pacific Ocean (Pac-IF-ic O-cean) the earth's largest body of water. It extends from the Arctic to the Antarctic and from the Americas to Asia and Australia.

papi (PA-pi) Spanish word for daddy.

penguin species (PEN-guin SPE-cies) the eighteen species of penguins range from the Galápagos Islands at the equator to Antarctica at the South Pole. The smallest penguin is the blue fairy penguin at sixteen inches (30 centimeters) tall. The largest are the emperor (EM-per-or) penguins at about four feet (120 centimeters) tall. Penguins live for about ten to twelve years in the wild and are thought to mate for life.

Pinnacle Rock (PINN-a-cle Rock) a tuff cone on Bartolomé Island. A tuff cone is a rock made of hardened ash. Ash is powdery bits of lava.

Sally Lightfoot Crab (SAL-ly LIGHT-foot crab) a bright red crab that can be seen on the black lava rocks of many of the Galápagos Islands. It's said that the crab was named after a dancer from the island of Jamaica.

snorkeling (SNORK-el-ing) a swimmer snorkeling uses a mask to see, a snorkel or tube to breathe, and foot-fins to swim underwater.

South America (South A-MER-i-ca) one of the seven continents (CON-ti-nents) or large bodies of land in the world. It is below North America.

South Pole the part of the earth that is the most southern.

warm-weather penguins There are four species of warm-weather penguins: The Magellanic penguin, the Humbolt (or Peruvian) penguin, the black-footed penguin, and the Galápagos penguin. While they live in different locations, they look and behave in many of the same ways.

Dear Parents and Educators:

Welcome to the Young Readers' series!

These learning stories have been created to introduce young children to the study of animals.

Children's earliest exposure to reading is usually through fiction. Stories read aloud invite children into the world of words and imagination. If children are read to frequently, this becomes a highly anticipated form of entertainment. Often that same pleasure is felt when children learn to read on their own. Nonfiction books are also read aloud to children but generally when they are older. However, interest in the "real" world emerges early in life, as soon as children develop a sense of wonder about everything around them.

There are a number of excellent read-aloud natural-science books available. Educators and parents agree that children love nonfiction books about animals. Unfortunately, there are very few that can be read *by* young children. One of the goals of the Young Readers' series is to happily fill that gap!

Penguins of the Galápagos is one in a series of learning stories designed to appeal to young readers. In the classroom, the series can be incorporated into literature-based or whole-language programs, and would be especially suitable for science theme teaching units. Within planned units, each book may serve as a springboard to immersion techniques that include hands-on activities, field study trips, and additional research and reading. Many of the books are also concerned with the threatened or endangered status of the species studied and the role even young people can play in the preservation plan.

These books can also serve as read-aloud for young children. Weaving information through a story form lends itself easily to reading aloud. Hopefully, this book and others in the series will provide entertainment and wonder for both young readers and listeners.

C.A.

Guidelines for the Young Readers' Series

In the Classroom

One of the goals of this series is to introduce the young child to factual information related to the species being studied. The science terminology used is relevant to the learning process for the young student. In the classroom, you may want to use multi-modality methods to ensure understanding and word recognition. The following suggestions may be helpful:

1. Refer to the pictures when possible for difficult words and discuss how these words can be used in another context.

2. Encourage the children to use word and sentence contextual clues when approaching unknown words. They should be encouraged to use the glossary since it is an important information adjunct to the story.

3. After the children read the story or individual chapter, you may want to involve them in discussions using a variety of questioning techniques:
   a. Questions requiring *recall* ask the children about past experiences, observations, or feelings. (*Have you ever seen movies or TV programs about Galápagos penguins?*)
   b. *Process* questions help the children to discover relationships by asking them to compare, classify, infer, or explain. (*Do you have to eat every day? Does the Galápagos penguin? Why or why not?*)
   c. *Application* questions ask children to use new information in a hypothetical situation by evaluating, imagining, or predicting.

At Home

The above aids can be used if your child is reading independently or aloud. Children will also enjoy hearing this story read aloud to them. You may want to use some of the questioning suggestions above. The story may provoke many questions from your child. Stop and answer the questions. Replying with an honest, "I don't know," provides a wonderful opportunity to head for the library to do some research together!

Have a wonderful time in your shared quest of discovery learning!

Carol A. Amato
Language-Learning Specialist